T0380630

SUBVERSIVE MINDS

PENETRATING A SACRED

THOT

DEPTHS OF PERVERSION AND RECONFIGURATION OF THE SOUL

FRANKIE NICOLE

SUBVERSIVE MINDS PENETRATING A SACRED THOT
DEPTHS OF PERVERSION AND RECONFIGURATION OF THE SOUL

iUniverse books may be ordered through booksellers or by contacting:

iUniverse
1663 Liberty Drive
Bloomington, IN 47403
www.iuniverse.com
844-349-9409

ISBN: 978-1-6632-3042-3 (sc)
ISBN: 978-1-6632-3041-6 (e)

Library of Congress Control Number: 2021921504

Print information available on the last page.

iUniverse rev. date: 01/05/2022

I dedicate this book to the hopeless romantics who forever believe in love and hope in all things good. This isn't a book of hate or to degrade anyone, it is a book a pure feelings and optimistic belief that we can manifest what we desire out of this world. There is just a need to get thoughts out on paper or spoken. There is however, a very special person that was held in my mind during many very powerful poems.

So here is to you:

I can't really understand my feelings for you, it is like there was an instant recognition of who you were to me. A kindred spirit, but deeper and far more intense. The day we met I had an instant spiritual high from just looking into your eyes. It took some time to further understand what that feeling was and would become, by far it is the most spectacular thing I have ever experienced. I hope everyone in life get to experience it. Although I understand some aren't as dramatic, existential, dramatic, wild or imaginative; there should be a desire to have love that makes your whole self feel. I see you and you see me, that is all that matters. I held love for you when you were with someone else who hurt you, and it hurt me to watch. But I could only burn for you. I want you and only you. This is my profession of love for you, my person.

Here is to the happiness in life. Peace.
Love, Frankie Nicole

CONTENTS

Chapter 1 Wounding 1

Devil's Snare 2

Dilation 3

Death becomes her 5

Cork Screwed 6

Tart Eulogy 7

Confusing the Waiting Game 9

Blood lust 10

Bloody Entrails Dragging 11

Death Becomes Him 12

Last Thoughts 13

Losing it 14

Wandering Hands 15

Enmeshment 16

High Dive 17

Inconceivable 19

Nerves 20

The fear of loss 22

The Pulse 24

Chapter 2 Purgatory 25

Dark Eternal Vibrations 26

Implausible Dreams 27

Expulsion 29

Fucking Screaming 30

Reconfiguring 32

Infusion of the Heart 34

Et. All 36

Faintly 38

Chapter 3 Regrowth 39

The Light 40
Breaking the Black Hole 41
Catch me 42
Soaring Hooves 43
Thorns 45
Crumbs 46

Chapter 4 Redemption 49

Trigger Points 50
Oh! Goddess! 51
Only Light 53
Deemed Royalty 54
Varnished Layers 55
Low Point 58
Glint 60
Deftly the white flag 61

Chapter 5 Inside Out 65

My Core 66
The mountain 67
Sour Note 69
Toxic Femininity 70
Body Talk 73
Perfect Timing 74
The Consistent Question 77
Taking Names 78
Again 79

CHAPTER 1

Wounding

@davesphotos.pnw

DEVIL'S SNARE

Temptation
All around
Much attention
To be found
I can touch and feel
But I know it isn't real
Powder fresh
Libations flows
Fresh growth of roses on a mound
Horned devils abound
But my thoughts only reflect of you
I wish you were here
I wish you were less stubborn
I wish I could always have my way
Sip my wine
Hoping to be fine
Cross my heart I'll keep my mind
Soon it'll be just us two
I promise I love only you

DILATION

Secrets, secrets
Lies
The eyes
They never lie

They may fib
They may skirt the line
Flash and spin
Flirt and dance about

But stare directly
And there is always truth

The wisdom
The knowledge
Of what is
What was
And what could be

The eyes that watch me
Veiled betwixt the sheets
I read everything in those eyes

Every flicker
Slowly
Explains it all

Are you looking at me?
I'm looking
I see

Do you see me
Or just through me
Am I transparent?

Flushing shade of chartreuse
When I show off my innards
Gory and gleaming

Screaming out loud
At the top of my lungs
Alone in gardens of my heart

Eyes
Shielded
Locked up to set free

Break me out of this cage
Flare in the dark forest
Tend to me with your stare

Those eyes

DEATH BECOMES HER

She is stiff
    Cold
No spirit
Waiting
To be put underground
There
The wasteland of her body
Nothing left to cherish
Next lifetime
You might have her
If you can find the one
That special one
That makes your heart go overboard
Beating out of the chest
Crying out in your sleep for her
For the one who makes sense
Who makes your soul yearn
You might know
If you really learned
But I don't know if you learned
I cannot teach
Had too many demanding pupils
You must feel it within
So again I say
Death becomes her
I shall return next time
For they have killed me
And now I must regenerate

CORK SCREWED

Twisting and turning
My spine crunches as the bones go adrift
Spinning out of control
From where it supports my body
Turgot's of measly flesh that hold me together

If I do not allow myself to fly
Holding the truth within my teeth
Brandishing it all for those to see
How will they know?
Who will come to my funeral?
Thanking me for all those things I once said
The blindfolds ripped off from the bloody sockets
Painfully showing what was before unseen
A process of eliminating
The clutter and the crust
That destroys humanity
Tearing those apart that wish to be
All because of permeated lie
What do I say?
When you've spit in my face
Cursed my name in the center stage
Wishing others to see the lowest of my character.

TART EULOGY

He calls me sweet.
Not endearing or literal like a cupcake
Or like my pussy, so good he can't take his lips away from.
But like:
"Aw you poor stupid, pathetic girl!"
Like my kindness is something to be ashamed of,
Like because I show vulnerability,
That somehow that makes me weak.
Shit, I've been bleeding monthly since I was twelve,
Who the fuck you think is weak?
Like because I don't right away point out all your flaws,
Malign any brave new idea,
Or take advantage of your need to feel a part of something
I must be soft...
Is my frailty showing, or just yours?
If you knew how many times I smiled instead of crying?
Those times when I wanted to slap someone for being such a creep,
When his hand moved far too close to private areas,
When the back door deal went to his buddy,
To be taken seriously as an artist,
But only 'sad faced' and raped.
It takes balls to be as strong as a woman
But balls are weak
So who own them
Turning around and torment those who don't put up an iron curtain.
Too afraid to embrace softness,
As patriarchy teaches them to kill anything nurturing.
So they do,
Inside themselves,
As well as in others.
With guns,
Available in all shades.
When they cannot,
They incarcerate.
There is a fine line between suspects and the real criminals,

Rocket man has to play a powerful game of swords.
My penis won't suffice, so here's some impressive CALORIMETRY!
You know what's sweet?
Kindness.
Persistence.
Patience.
Hope.
Optimism.
Somewhere we've lost virtues in the quest to impress,
Tired of this class slavery.
The serfdom that never left,
If the solution is as easy as looking within.
Assuaging our egos to take a moment,
Self-reflecting on why we are so afraid of our time here.
When we circle lifetimes again and again.
Sometimes you are the clot,
Others, the artery.
Remembering someday dessert is served.

CONFUSING THE WAITING GAME

As she sat there perplexed by her current situation
Not knowing which way to go,
No moves left to make
Nothing but to sit there and wait.
Not a moment she was quite use to.
More like woman of action.
Stagnation was not a comfort level
She lacked a stable footing, her ground trembling beneath her usually stable feet
If she cried out for mercy who would answer the call
Would she want someone to answer?
Could she afford the feeling of vulnerability?
Allowing another hand at the control panel.
To trigger hidden emotions that she dodged consistently.
What was she to do?
The idea to succumb to those feelings that could alter the beast of her being.
Too close to the heater and her fingertips might singe.
Blister up and tinge with the sharp pain of the physical plane.
That was real.
The pain, only a side effect of the excitement
Is abstract and cannot be caught up in earthy realities.
She didn't feel comfortable there,
How to behave and hold herself.
Indisposed, un-composed, like a contained symphony waiting to be written.

BLOOD LUST

Abandoned me again for foolish pride
I simmer alone
Yet, I am alright alone
Come to my peace with aloneness
We are alone in this life
From birth to death
I miss you though
To be object of your desire
The one your mind cannot release
A trap of neuronic synapses
Lighting up an EEG
I ache for you
If only I was next to you
My body lightly doused in the after glow
Waves of your energy flowing
You hurt me
Disconnected the chord
Shredded my spine
Left dangling dinner of wolves
Near death
For dearly departed
Why?
Why do you do me so wrong?
What have I done to deserve such a wrung?
Take the knife from my neck
Your wild look
That rings in your pupil
Is not from me
Blood gushing from the lips
I am not to blame
Please do not assert your blood lust on my psyche
Take the blade from my throat
Do not break me for the pains that others have brought you
Love me because I have shown you that you are loved

BLOODY ENTRAILS DRAGGING

I cannot give you hope
The pulse is weak
Self-fulfilling prophesy
Afforded you an extra life
From my own manifested
Price has been listed
Done what can, DNR
Lacking what will with a bill
Depleted from the weight
Strong, but not carrying the both of us
Now only debt to be paid
Must find the strength to forge on
I only know my part
Come back, that is up to you
Misfortune and the blessing to see potential
Jump too quick then fall without a net
Only left is my shadow
Do they realize I have gotten away?

DEATH BECOMES HIM

Here on earth
We mere mortals
exist as a reflection of the space gods
To experience who we are in different dimensions
To feel the connection of another human
To enjoy the simple pleasures
As the sad simple beings, we be
Pity us as you will but we pity you
Floating around with nothing and no one to hold on to
Pacifying your existence pulling the tendrils of others
Toying unconquered with lives
Never really living
Never really dying
Stuck suspended
To evolve is to die
As painful as it is.
Those brave enough to take a dip into depths of feelings
Welcomed with creatures and pathways unseen
You may think you know it all
Detached from the foolishness we vapid mortals enjoy
Yet, yet
That is the sting of the ego
Stunting your perpetual motion
Suffocating your dreams
Stifling your hopes
Magnifying your fears
Existence is to balance in between space and earth
Not avoid it like a coward
Reach for the stars
Not reside in mode
Your mortality is calling
Are you ready to die?

LAST THOUGHTS

I realize my pain
Clouded judgement
Of what is true:
For the seed to grow
She must be willing
Willing to accept the task
He introduces to her
For he is the one who recognizes
A mirrored soul before him
However
Wherever the path leads
Must reconcile
Before she accepts her mission
Lighting up the world
With gold
Power and self
Raising the consciousness of others
Leading the way, they rein
She the expansion
The vessel
He the control
The initiator
Beloved they
Forever be
Combined together
Combusted in collision
Conquered hearts

My heart is ripped open.
Drowning in emotion.
It waits only for thee.
My sanctimonious broken king.
Feline's intuition.

LOSING IT

Don't give a hoot
Could not stop thinking of you with all my might
Underestimating the longing in my words?
Feel the fast-flourishing flush of my fire?
The needs, the wants.
Superficiality does not have weight here.
Frightening unknown as pieces of my soul exposed
Completely vulnerable
Read deeper
Reach deeper
Go deeper
Consume me before the flames of my yearning overwhelm this gentle constitution of mine
Subdermal contact burns
I want your eyes to say yes
Then your lips
Only the best inspires the best of me

WANDERING HANDS

Hands off
Hands on
Hands off

Where do they go
Found my body
Found the mother sprawled out

Taking it with you
When you leave
How I am possessed

Daemons inside
Outside in
Snipping pieces of me

Shake my spine
Ensconce me
Dreams made

Dreams lost
The sprites bright over my bed
Dangling, as if on strings

Twinkling in my eyes
Swirls trace the sulci of my hippocampus
Stiff as a board

Paralyzed
I want
No! I desire
Hands on

ENMESHMENT

Allowed himself to look at her face
Examined every little inch of it
From a bump to a grooved wrinkle
Small and insignificant
Yet leaving a marring
Seeing the significance of life
Times of sorrow
Times so high and bright
The only thing unseen
The numbness
An empty void
How often did that swallow her?
How often did she seek it?
An escape from reality
From the mundane and tragic
Yet so innocent
Who could know?
She didn't say much about her feelings
He looked
Peered into the dilated pupils
Searching
For any insignificant shred of hope
All he wanted was to know
Did she care?
Did she want him?
Did she love him?

HIGH DIVE

I find myself
On the cusp
Of something new

Daunting
Taunting
Into the unknown

Trepidations
Peer forward
Am I ready?

Leading into the wilderness
Abandonment
Of sanity

    Am I prepared?
Survivalist packed?

Will I ever really be?
Always will have to be
Ultimately
Prepared
For an exception

I want
I want so bad it hurts
With ever cell of me
Screaming, yelling
Torn between safety and a free fall

Gut twisting unstoppable lightness of plunge

DO I DARE???
For love
The final frontier
Truly solemnity to trust another
Fully
With the hand the hard
Heart
Pressed and squeezed
Pulled and stretched
Blead and emptied of what is, was, and would be
Sometimes
We look for a reason
Sometimes the reason finds us

Reasonable
Reasonless
How to know
Hand over eyes
Once leg extended
I step

INCONCEIVABLE

It is
For us
To be together
Imaginary wistful wish
A fantasy of fantasies
Where I build myself
A magic bridge to your broken kingdom
Where sorrows of past heartaches do not exist
But that is
A paradox
Because lacking pain
Pleasure does not exist
Knowing that I can't have you now
Allows me the pleasure to love the very idea of you
Every kiss we haven't had
Every caress of tingling skin
I adore the memory
Unattainable
I have just the reality of hate and war
Love is the only antidote
Love
Love
Love
Is the answer
What is your question?

NERVES

My heart leaps into my chest every time I hear the door sway
My stomach churns as if a million creepy crawly things inhabit it
Nearly void of course
Twice
I don't mean to be cowardly
But loving you makes me weak
My knees
My elbows
Grounded when I am called
Am I ready?
Capable or culpable
Verbalize
Say my piece without falling to pieces
Waiting for the hour

Extended time and I fear you've abandoned me
My heart
Such the fragile heart
That took the leap and tried to believe
Is souring with each minute you are not here
You spurn me
You burn me
Real tears,
Not whimpering simple manipulations
The first real tears cried in a decade
Wounded grave and unimaginable depths
Recovery?
Burdens borne long time held
Not the bridge nor tunnel
To be more feral,
I would burn your forest pillage your village and destroy the kingdom
But I know the better thing is just to walk away.

Unlike any other, yet
Cheap and easy with my love
Presumptions have a great cost
I am lost
Sobbing
You have broken my heart
For that there is no cure

You do not own my power for it is only my own.
Lost vulnerability shared, now I am just
A ghost

THE FEAR OF LOSS

Not taking a step toward
Something you've hoped for
Yet also fear the failure
Why though?
Does past predicate future action?
Repetitive behaviors lead us in a loop
The misconceptions of a misunderstanding
Standing still as the world changes around
What are you so afraid of?
What if we fail…. but what if we fly?
Made it this far
Seems as if we have resolve to fix the cracks with gold.
The heart
Quivering
Strong yet fragile
Tempestuous frontings for soft soul
Face to face with the possession of her own desires
Afraid to lose all of herself
Into demonic possession.
I want so badly
To take a leap
Blindfolded stepping off the cliff
The death of many seem to make me brave
Thinking again, that I might not see your face
Feel the slow supple moves
Suck on your fingers.
Do you love me enough to step out from behind the wizard's curtain?
What if we only had today?
What if we only had the past?
Wasted it with petty quibbles?
I would rather spend the future with you
In a love nest

Time is not a virtue for all
We must act today
We must act now
Be brave, I promise to be too.
Adieu Mi Amore

THE PULSE

What speaks this heart
When there is nothing left
When it has burst forth
Bloodied and beaten
Transformed
For the Danzig
Dressed in gilded curls
Not knowing
Now wanting
But needing
Every drop of pain
To push forward
Forth for the likes of love
Without salt in the wound
How does it grow
How does it know
Crown of leaves
Crown of thorns
All the same to me
If only to grasp for a second
That who swells my heart
Too large for my body
Making for a gagged target
Fickle strings plucked
Joyous and tragic all the same
As we die laying
Twisted
Extremities
Consisting as everlasting infinite
A passing moment of pleasure it gives us
Forever etched

CHAPTER 2

Purgatory

@ianphares

DARK ETERNAL VIBRATIONS

Prince of darkness
Slithering snake!
Wormed your way through my heart
Leaving holes and putrid puss
Oh silly prince
Little do you know
I have no heart
It was already eaten
Not a delight for you to devour
A lost soul of sorts
Finding no root to grab
I am limitless
Limited
Took me by the throat
Waved me around
Limp bodied wafting flag
Untended flesh
At your whim, sir
Just here to look pretty
Thought you had me
But no one has me
I got them
Read them
I see to, become them?
'Tis the life in ethereal
I wish it wasn't so
I wish I could submit
But it will never be
So, I bid adieu
Adieu
Forever in my dream
You will be
Leader, oh a king you
A brazen rose queen, I
I love you,
Eternally.

IMPLAUSIBLE DREAMS

Dreamed you up so long ago
Waiting
Sighing
I've pined for you
I lost track in time
Lashing pain with hope
Lessons came to unground my doubt
A set up to undo unrealistic expectations

Brought me to you
Landed unpredictably in my lap
Calm and cool, collected
No walking anxiety with you
Just sitting together as ourselves
Heard the expression of heartfelt love for me
Indirect, yet knowing it was meant for me
I was taken back by the candid statement made
Last time someone stated it too soon, such a disaster
To think someone would say that so soon again,
Not sure I was ready
I was unlovable at the time,
Past wounds held barriers to present
Wanting to believe but finding the will out of reach
But one of us had to be strong, save the day
Dismayed thinking you had to save me
I am a stature of my own strength and influence
I don't know what gave me the strength
Carrying my lifeless body to the end of the journey
I couldn't stand not having you in my life
A power disadvantage of imposturous proportions
Yet the struggle ensued

Tell me how much I am needed in your life
Saving myself from loneliness,
Begging to know that we are loved.

You've been trying to tease me,
Driving me crazy
Coo-coo coco poofs
In the bag waiting for a hand
Like the floor is falling out from under me
Give me your undying commitment and devotion
So loud and proud
Give it all to me
Your time and attention,
High priority for someone of high honor
Lest the assholes demand your time and leave such misery

No longer can I keep things hidden
Forced hand to expose the deep, deep depths of softest emotions
I've fought so hard to keep myself safe in the cocoon
To be vulnerable
This chance only comes around once in a lifetime
A catch, not to be put on a shelf or taken for granted
Unmatched connections must be recognized
Painting the moon and stars together
This is our lifetime
Shatter the mold and making the amazing happen.

We can go the distance
Half in tangible realities
Others fractured within the subtle feels
My twin and a soulmate
Could not be ashamed or embarrassed to say
But to reveal it?

My beautiful soul,
Relinquish the devil that binds
Ignite with me
Clean up the soul, I believe in you
I love you
I want only you
Can't live without anymore

EXPULSION

Everything I once numbed
Now leaks out of me
When it was easier not to feel
I coated it with varnish to pretend it was so pretty
That is why I hold people
Because I know how it feels to be hurt
By those you trust
We're all just looking for someone to care
Some are unfit for the job
We become self-reliant
Hoping to hold ourselves up
But what then, when it all becomes too much
Do we dance and drown our sorrows with frivolity?
Meaningless sexual trysts
With those who can't look us in the face tomorrow
Clinging to our friends until they must leave us
How to step over the walls?
Barricades of safety to ward off dark night predators
Trudging forward into the wilderness
For comfortable alone has become
Comfortably disconnected
Carefully distracted
Longing for the touch of that person who will wake you from a dream
Paddling in the deep pools of our subconscious mind
Not afraid to peer into the water
The boogie man is only as bad as the unknown characters he plays
Can they keep me from drowning?
Or will they push my head under and swim away?
To revive love there must be clarity
For how many of us swim in the dark
Can I trust you to help me saw off this anchor?
Every human for themselves, then?
Fool me once
Fool me twice
Shame, shame, shame on me.

FUCKING SCREAMING

I loathe this feeling
The lack of control I have
My heart like a floundering guppy
Tossed up on to the shore

    Gasping

So much movement
Too quick for the jellied candy heart of mine
Comforted by a large shell
Forced to find itself a new abode
How quickly?
On quicksand
With no bottom
And the drop
I need security
A handle to clutch
Subtle manipulations that carry the reins I am so comfortable holding
Like ripping off skin
Raw and blotched bloody

    I shiver
    Not just lightly
    A violent shudder arose to shake the soul
    Jaw clenched
    Blacked out
    Swirling, swirling
    If I hate this does it conversely mean I love it?
    Or am I just overturned in the surf
    Gasping for air

Mixed up in the cruel tricks of puppetry and slide of hand
Get your paws out of me
I am not here to play
Rules and boundaries, are you not following?

I did not take a fall because I enjoy scraped knees
Showing that I too, am human
    An air of vulnerability
For arms to fold around me
Hearts to reach out
That I bleed the same too

RECONFIGURING

You want to be a work of art?
I will take that as a yes
When you try to play my heart
Pretending until the end
Amusing playthings
Lovers for a night
Whether in my daydreams
Or deep in rem sleep tonight
Not so obvious
But deeply in the ephemeral
Repetitions, when and how
A mask of attentiveness
A fated fatal attraction if you must
Looking at me as he licks his lips
A magnet between our bodies
You see how conflicted yet keen I become
In your presence I am weak in the knees
Soft in the throat
So, I whispered silently in my head
Through my eyes I shoot my shot
Helps when the peanuts squawk louder
I am stealth
Sweet secrets and hot sheets
Snatched the sweet cream of the crop
Words like a vampire sucking blood
From your femoral vein
Circulating spiritually above your body
Like nightmares of the sweetest dream
Projecting confidence unto the wanting mouth
Feed me
The cries of baby chicks
Mewing mad cats
Roaring dragons clinging to gold
Beware my pointed arrow
She stands firm steady hand

Obey or die.
You may live with one exception
Amend
Grovel
Show me your humility
As quick as a beckoning eye
Freezes you to stone
Punishment isn't even enough
You coward!
As she rips off his head with her bare teeth
The same used to bite and bruise
The truth may sting
But deranged?
I do believe you are mistaking me
For a bitch who gives a damn.

INFUSION OF THE HEART

Can you feel my heart?
It lights up with heat
Infused by a sober breath

Essence danced slowly
Tracing my skin barrier

A pulse heightens
Like those primal organs
Leaping into the throat

Dreary days return
In your absence

The rain rips open
Pockets of the skies
Pouring down tragic tears

The barometer stands
Lower than most
Dreams, Fantasies
Dividing me into two

With the strength
In my passions I am raw

Like liquid that escapes
Invisible cracks

Dripping slowly to the floor
A hazardous goo
Endangering those who
Remain unaware

I yearn
I mew
I falter
I fawn

To love is to die slowly
One million times over

Cells of skin that aid
Regeneration
The hearts electric connection
Peels me away slowly

Rendering all docile and still
I love to die every time you are near

ET. ALL

I want it all
The good, divine, and exquisite
The bad, mundane, and everyday
The ugly, vile, putrid and rotting

Should anyone steal you from me
Surely, I would die
My heart would seize up
Crumble out of my body
I would fall shriveled and dead before ever hitting the ground

A brief yet thorough haunting
This time I'll just leave
From the bottom up, begin again
Until the next lifetimes in formation
Meet me again, to have this love on replay
Rejoin the opposition of souls

I know you want me, all of me.
An inkling of intuitive nudges
Reflection of a soul so alike genuinely
The search just as thorough as mine
Desire to meet your match just as strong
Chord connected deep from your heart to mine

Chains cannot be dismantled
Bonds not broken
Love is on the table
Pull up a seat

Like a misted rose
Blossomed and at the precipice of its peak
I will not pluck you from the ground and keep you
Nor you will with I
For the spirit will die prematurely

No, no
I will grow beside you
We will grow together

My best friend, lover
Always in my heart

FAINTLY

Softly
Sturdy
Take it slow
Take your time
One beat after another
Patiently
Find me waiting there
At a crossroads
Left
Right
Right
Left
Crossing the boundaries of illusion and control
One step closer
One step back
Finding the wholeness
Was here all along
Be silent my sweet
For nothing says it all
The universe speaks
With the glory for timing
The beauty in small
The pause
The halt
Sweetness only abides by the rules

CHAPTER 3

Regrowth

@lockephoto

THE LIGHT

I can see you
Transduced between layers
Peeled back
Sliced away the noise
Turbulent vibrations that distract
The pine of pines
Fresh green and fertile
New growth leaks out of every crack
Meshed and mixed
Germinated from the multitude of seeds
Effervescing illumination
The rest of the world waits for me to impress them
But you see I just am
Impressive
Expanding
Loving
Pure
Without presence
My special gift

BREAKING THE BLACK HOLE

My heart, my heart
Love of all my lifetimes
Saving it all just for you
Every lesson I've learned
Every experience I felt
Prepared me to meet you now
Just as through your life
Has and will
Prepare you for
The gloriousness that is me
Together we will make magic
Glorious musical ingenuity
Greater than anyone has ever promised before
Because we know
And have known
What it is
The eyes, they never lie
My sweet, my dear my love
Just some time longer
Until I get to hold you in my arms
When the cosmos collide
A supernova
The reverb will be felt for millennia to come

CATCH ME

The distance
Traveled
By me
Is not in question
I've been here in the background
Waiting for you
Helping you
Secretly
Playing those games, we play
Passing time to keep in touch
Rock the boat
We claim so innocent
With pushing boundary lines
Pop off of sparks
To tease or tempt a move
All leading to
A path we don't know the end of
But it seems
That we want to do it together.
So, tell me
Is that your goal?
Seeking answers?
To the end of all time?
As long as it takes, I figure

SOARING HOOVES

My enduring love, oh lover
Followed by phantoms
Do not avert me my love
Find me
Face to face
Cheek to cheek
Ignite the small bumps of flesh
That are stimulated by the softest touch
Peel the droplets of sweat off my skin with your tongue
Vein by vein
Counted
All are plumped and erect
Pulsing
Soaring
Blood percolating a million cells a minute
Oxygen transferred into energy
Breath quickens
Beats tricky
Off and on
On and off
As if they were controlled by a short switch
I am no longer in control
Swimming
Mewing
Mailing
Misaligned
Flushed with a fever
Heat waves rise off pounds of me
Lost within
No longer present

Lover, oh friend
Build me a tower to peer over all
Will you invite me to join you?
Over air waves

Among trees
Riding through the night
Weary and lone
Communing
Vibrating in the ear
Input will return
Another screen and I will scream
Touch, I must be touched
Onward ride I must
Heavy handed and caught throat
Enough is enough
Even fools find a different journey

Lifetime to a space in time
Grand scheme of it all
Appears answers
Sat in trepidation
Knowing if I must
Seeker of the finer touch
Wasting time in the waiting line
Is it ever really wasted?
No real connection
To whom I speak
Emptiness becomes the weight of the world rested upon me
No longer abide on the emptiness
I must fill this cup
I will fill this cup
Hope fills up this cup

THORNS

The roses
Oh the roses
Neither you nor I own the roses
They do not connect us per se
It is a happenstance
That I am the queen of thorns
And you wear them around your heart
Thus is not us a couple made
Tragically
Romeo thinks Juliet is dead
Departs ignorantly thinking there is nothing left
She, transformed into someone who determinedly knows
How to handle the intense emotions in the flow
Direct her magic
Her projections of adoration to her beloved
Love only in the mind of she
Everything given is a reflection of her love for herself
Only a similar understanding
Symbiotically joining with that what she wishes to project
Hatred, shame, sorrow disconnects that which could have been joyous
For how long?
Who knows
This we do know
That each person has a path to traverse
So until then
My friend
Oh secret lover
An old reflection
Refract away the angles of disturbance
Untangle from my soul
Find me anew
Rebirthed
Returned

CRUMBS

If you love someone
You'll let it be
The power of it all
Fractious quibbling
Grabbing
Consuming
Draining
Lenny
Mouse in hand
Being ever so
Vulnerable
Despite which position
Here we are
Can't say what I want to
Forgot it's not allowed
Only good for the dance
Pay attention?
What if
What if you don't
What if it doesn't
I know why
Stigmatized
Friendliest zoned
Blank place
Wasted
Feeling used
OH my feelings
Were really never anyone else's
Gotta learn
Don't hurt your own feelings
Silently
I hold on
Whatever the manufactured dream
Dreamt so many dreams
But really love

Not my religion
Way of life
No deity to kiss ass
No people to hate
Not even ignorance
I tried
Better to be compassionate
And let them fall
On their own dumbass sword
All goal posts on a different timeline swirling throughout space
I'm worried I might lose you
Again
I might be too picky
Unrealistic
Not nice
Overbearingly smothering
Mask that I wear
Unprotected
You from me
The annoying imperfections
Making me unlovable
Circle back into desperation
Heaving hard or makes the thread unravel
Instead of wrapped in warmth
Naked and exposed
Next to a clump of material
So hard to be vulnerable
With such an easy target
I tiptoe in pieces
Crumbs
Match your cadence
Because I'm afraid
I'll be holding my end
All alone.

CHAPTER 4

Redemption

@lockephoto

TRIGGER POINTS

My dear sensitive soul
Take the brunt of my words too deep
Stirred within my heart a cauldron that needs a steady warm hand
Beholden
Pointed right side
Your creative mind has too much freedom to roam into the darkness
For I am the flame to glow in the blackest of nights
Breathe me in I will illuminate your world
Take the blinds off and you will see the warmth all around you
Do not sit in judgment of yourself
We all make mistakes
A slighted heart can have a sharp tongue
Only the pain from previous love pushes beloved away
Longing to bury my head into your chest and be cradled
An unhuman desire that takes a hold of my entire being
Not to be shaken for hell or high water

OH! GODDESS!

Oh goddess
What am I to do?
I've lost control
Mesmerized by you
Lawd!
Boy got a hold on me
Don't know how to tell you
So I keep it on the low
Becoming harder
Not to love you
But maybe it's
Just a little crush
Obsessions
Come easy to me
The low lights
Keeps not all sights to be seen
Rush
Oh just a little rush
Of blood to my hushh.
Keep it all covered up
But I can't stop
With just a little touch
Sending me on a quaking spine
Might just have to make you mine
Under neath the glow
Moonlight view
Though I keep my cool
Wish you would make a move
In bed all day
Cuddled next to you
Bring you all the sauce
Get freaky

Big daddy one day
Soft kitty tomorrow
Let's play
Endless possibilities
With my mate
Best friend
Homeslice
Partner and in crime

ONLY LIGHT

Shadows of night
I peer curiously over
Not everything is clear
But I can feel it
The tension in the room
So potent I can taste it
Who moves first?
A standoff
Between lovers
And friends
I don't need you
But I want you to want me
There's a brick in my chest
Welling with such melancholy
Staring down the fear
Find what you desire
Open myself up
In the most intimate way
Because here I am
Showing that
Vulnerability
Whip of the Neck
So close you can feel
The beating pulses
That which reminds us
We're alive
To dive deep and multiply
Little parts of who we are
At any given place and time
The question is
Do I trust you enough?
Put the full essence into the tiger's mouth
Do I?

DEEMED ROYALTY

King, oh my king
Honorable, just and kind
Thoroughly all that you are
Leader of man
Master of just the one
Keeper of miserable misers and knaves
I do not place my own judgment on your choices
Beauty is pure
Love, respect and honesty
In equal exchange.
Malicious, unkind, unwelcome in this bond
Connection persists without touch or proximity
Pleasures free from toxicity
Only love and joy
Forever in flux
Harmonious alchemy of fire, water, earth, and air
Steamy, reactive, and exciting
Stirring the animal nature within
My heart, not just an organ of flesh and blood
But the vessel of which my desire emanates
Cool, calm, soft, enveloping
Elemental purity of the combustion that with each beat continues the life force allowing it
Hot, searing streams of energy travel through each vein, vessel and artery.
Distinguishing it, life from death itself
Falling back into consciousness energy translates to though emoting frequencies that are received
You receive me.
I receive you.
My Royal.
And I be your Royal.

VARNISHED LAYERS

Who am I supposed to be?
Unbecoming, what is expected
So easy to just conform
Stuff myself into some low-rise jeans
Well, he likes it when I...
Don't you know she's a...
But this how it's always been.
Just a burden of personal demands
Oppressing to repress
Weaving fibers of an impossible feat
For people to just exist.
Don't be too loud, you'll scare people
You shouldn't speak your mind
What if someone judges ME for it
What a poor reflection of ME
Rejection projection
What will people think about ME?
If they hear you
Or comprehend anything you say
Narrowed in from a small peep hole
Careful, not too nude
Clutches them pearly whites
Linked to you? Never!
Because you're a "liability"
To my ego...

Hey, hey look!
Look, this girl obeys
She had molded herself well
Peak performance
Of my ideal expectations
Like plastic
Or a mannequin doll,
Poised for the perfect pussy
Cold fish

Haven't had a hug in weeks
Skin deep,
How do I turn off this doubt?
Why do you have to make this so difficult?!
Why can't you just be normal?
Why can't you just obey?
Behave
Be this
Be less
Be.
Be silent.
Do I look like a receptacle?
Have I become your waitress?
The entitlement
Of expecting someone to change for you
Accommodate so you don't dim their shine
Oppress to fit your box of horrors and deeds
Hold back so that the others can fly high
Can I run away screaming now?
Fleeing from judging jealousy
Ego
We're all smart in our own ways,
My intelligence isn't overwhelming
You might just be intimidated.
Why must I be something else?
Don't you want to know me?
Accept me for who I am
Why have you already decided
I don't fit
Linear thinking in a 5D world
Only angles here
Pay attention!
Too many positions to even contemplate

I'm not going to keep giving access
My time is expensive
No attention to be paid
Registering what I've brought to the table
Subtle and sweetness

Needs a refined and trained eye
They want me!
But at the expense of me
No masters, no gods
My own keeper
Parlay or piss off
Forcing my hand
To become a tolerable presence
Guarantees they silently resent you
In control of the game
A building a pit of rage to consume
Abusing ever part of good
Until it crumbles into yet another failed disaster

LOW POINT

They saw you at a low
Laughter, pity, ire
Thought they'd see the end
Watching for a grand "finale"
Plotting your demise
Lying in wait to see a failure
But little do know
Realize or understand
Highs and lows
Come naturally to you
Perhaps small minds lack full dimension
The only pleasure derived from others pain
Waiting in the squalor
Matrix of bodies writhing in filth
"Join us…" they moan
Relinquished of standards and drive
Give in to the pressure
Spinning webs of entanglement and lies
"We are the new way forward"
They retort
"It doesn't get better than this"
Echoing long stories past
"Settle for what you have"
Lest you know what is coming next
Babe, they can't even fathom your vision
The way your eyes sparkle
Ideas of grander
No, just a smoking pipe dream
But true innovation
You are GOD among the mortals
Don't forget to rip off your shirt every now and again
Feel the blood pumping through your chest
Down to the loins
A hormonal crux that grabs the neck scruff
Hand delivered will to succeed

Pure heart, the only effective mirror
Covered lips do lie to protect the insecure
Talk of the town to keep a townie
Slice those ties to who was once standing
Replace fables with the rock-hard reality
Known and unknown
You are the master of your own act
Intermission?
Hell, I'm just getting started
Take a seat
Pay my fee
Contact Boundaries
Shut up and listen
Because now,
I'm here to take you on a magical journey
Where the only interludes
Are musically inclined
Pumped with adrenaline
And naked.

GLINT

The limerence of
Wish versus
Sobering reality
Is harsh on the senses
Stuck between
Desire and
Tangible
Skimming on skin
Lovely blankets
Comfort places
Things being venusy
Please let me live in
Your world
Take a ride into my psychic side
Walk my lines
The dance
Of tra la la
Beautimus
Ten of libations
Liberating us
From cheek to cheek
I breathe your breath
Chin to cheek
Lips do touch
I can only pretend to
Give you mouth to mouth
If it's not really kissing
But oh how I want to
Bite your lips and show
But I wait patiently
Until the time
Is right

DEFTLY THE WHITE FLAG

Defeated
It happens to the best
My heart
Feels so closed
So many misdirects
A lie that resounds
Echos
You want to believe
Someone who acts
Talks
Says trustworthy things
Is real
Why would you lie?
Maybe I'll learn
Really though ask yourself
Why do you need to lie?
What scares you
So much about the truth?
You've hurt me
1,2 punch in the gut
That don't mean you're
Big daddy
Ain't shit
With out consent
Men taking advantage
Of young girls
Power blinds
But who really has
The upper hand?
I don't want
The branch
If it is rotten
Flip it on the head
If I am stone
You can't penetrate

My soul
I'd rather choke
Myself
Than stomach
Any more ego
I have no more
To feel
Just walk away
Victory is meaningless
With you
No one wins
Showing only charming
People love the smile
Control freak lives within
Holding me
Withholding what once
Was given
Leaving me begging
For the original
So tricky
Fake
Almost evil
Do I believe intentions
Did you mean to hurt me
Accidentally
Or?
Dare I believe
This person I love
Wants to hurt me
Break down
All what was good
By playing
The victim
Sucker for
A lover who needs love
Sadly then
I'm the dumb dumb
Blamed for falling
Vulnerable

To someone I believed in
Now all I do
Is walk around in suspect
Never fully letting
A guard down
So when you wonder why
She isolates
Seems so miserable
Won't let you close
You leave
It's too hard
Why try with you
Reconfirmed
Her suspicions
You weren't worth it
Talk to your brothers
Call on your friends
Ask of them
Do better
Stop hurting one another
Stop allowing
Such poor behavior
Cause you're better than that

CHAPTER 5

Inside Out

@butterflyengine

MY CORE

I'm in love with you
I always have been
It just took me a while to get here
You're so hot
Like, I see you and damn
You are perfect just the way you are
You better be careful girl
Ima get you pregnant
But like you're also funny
Quick witted
Like, actually funny
Poised
And you listen
Comprehend
A treasure to be found
I can't believe there is someone like you
Get me, you just know
Feel as if I've known you all my life.
I am so in love
Definitely
Definitely, in love
Withstanding challenges
Doubt
Up against a wall
Defending course
Worth it
Totally worth it
Ima lock you down
Keep this
Forever.

THE MOUNTAIN

Walking away from bullshit
This week like.
Are you really that lazy?
Are you so focused on your own success.
That you'd sacrifice others
Rude
Who are you miss entitled?
Muttering under your breath at me
Oh, you'd punch me in the face?
Petty violence begets violence
I am a tree
Deep roots and harmonious leaves
But I am also the mountain
I boil deep within
Under the layers of dirt, you threw
I am GAEA
You wanna fuck with me?
I'll blow your ass up
With my hot, hot magma
Get fucked you dumb a$s ho3
Sitting dormant
Lying in wait
Tricky, tricky
Engulfing you with branches until you've disappeared
Sad, pathetic, slovenly
Leech
Not even adding any social grace
Or kindness to any situation
Filthy garbage vomited from your lips
Sour and staining everything around you
I'll let you slip and fall in your own mess
Nothing needed on my part

I am the empress
I am the tree
I am just sitting here waiting and watching
You fall on your own sword
Thinking I was stupid
Projecting your depth of vision onto me
Because all you care about is your selfish ass self.
Poor character is never becoming.
So, I just sit and wait for the wheel to turn
Karma in my favor this time.
Toodles!
See ya never!

SOUR NOTE

The things you say
How they sting
Like searing hot metal
Edged up in the inner thigh
Elongated session on the ribs
Why do you act like that?
Pretend to ignore my feelings
Such a fucking bitch
Do not ever grab me like that again
None of you is, as entitled as you act
Go ahead, project all over me
I suppose I can take it
Pity me for not choking your choices
Yet envy my progress
Elevating into the air
So high
So high
I'm walking on clouds
Activating goddess status
You could have the tools
If you bothered to activate yourself
Not just rely on someone to carry you
Then it's toxic
I can't waste my energy on you
It's like dumping into an endless pit
Needy wanting mouth all the time
Without any respect
Like you don't even give a shit about me
So why should I?

TOXIC FEMININITY

Unkind
Misappropriated
Misdirected words
Cut me off while I'm talking?
Ignore me speaking up
Boom, boom!
Bang, bop!
Here I come to burst your bubble
Excuse you
I see you now
shoving your butthole in my face
Stealing my ideas and practice as your own
Diminishing me in the process
Jealous?
Yeah, dream on
You can never be me
But you get to be you
And I guess that's ok?
Focused on my goals
Glow up to show up
I didn't waste time on frivolous things
Direct and focused
To the point
Sharpened up and poof
Here is my sword
Swallow it or face worse
Sparkle, sparkle, bitch
And yes, I am looking at myself in the mirror
You know, while you go on about yourself
Not that you're not interesting
Train wrecks are hard to look away from.
Oh, was that too harsh?
I'm sorry, would you like to fix your life?
Show me the money
You know,

So, I can eat!
Intellectual property ain't free
Keep chugging though
Choo, choo motherfucker
Here comes the train
Sooo judgmental
I see your eyes dart
Telling a story
More high ground
The "alpha" female
False confidence of fitting into an expectation
Undercutting and stealing to hold down others
Careful you don't fall off your pedestal, dear
Lest you might be down here with us mortals
Such flawed creatures
Hope you don't scare easy
I drag you along out of willingness
The kindness of friendship
No woman left behind
Upon arrival,
You're there: squawking a distraction
Boasting about how you made it
No acknowledgement of my hard work
I can't speak to you in truths?
No nursemaid or bitch here
Rejected from my life
Unworthy of my nurturing
Sit your bony ass down and take notes
Credit where it's due
Without me
You'd still be fucking different cocks every night
Choking on dick as not to think
Bemoaning "all men are trash!"
You are what you eat sweetie
Or hidden under your comforter
In tears slobbering
"Why am I stuck?"
Probably because you lack internal compassion for anyone including yourself.
Playing victim and victor in one sentence

Let's not split hairs
Who is the deity here?
Selfless ain't real
More like self-involved
Self-aggrandizing
Input needs a source
Here's looking at me kid.
Good luck to you though,
You're going to need it

BODY TALK

Am I svelte enough for you?
How you like me with curves?
Or do I reflect back
A version of self-love that you hate.
Yes, I know I am beautiful
I make a deafening sound when I walk
But not from bent floorboards
Not the sound of my clapping thighs
My body is none of your business
Talk about its shape
Solid food in the mouth
Skimpy stretched things over sturdy hips
My autotomy is that I make the final call
So please
Step off bitch
I don't care for your side coaching
For you are slave to outside sources
The approval of others
Monkey mind
Spinning hamster on the wheel
Gotta look better
Must improve
Or I will lose my sculpted power
That given to me by those
Who wish to knock me off
That pedestal we all sit on
Needing approval that we
In fact are attractive
Possibly worthy
For someone who is not equip to handle
All of these goodies
So put your milk shake to the streets
Put out a milky streak
I live freely
Only here to please myself

PERFECT TIMING

Every moment lead us back here
Where time has no direction or consistency
Unlocking a divine pathway
Slowly uncovering a passionate mystery
Glimpses of the golden desire

I saw it then, misty and brief
Unsure of what truly was
Following symbols and signs
Neon or more subtle

I've apologized enough for what wasn't my fault
However, I did lie
I wrote a letter but omitted the most important detail
I could have written you a whole book of my love

But would you have accepted it, me?
Afraid of your life
What was out of my control
Not considering the complexity of mine

Maybe we were both lying
Ignoring the red-hot elephant in the room
Because it was easier than opening up
A false sense of security holding on to a secret

Fear, with liquor on her lips
Eyes, that cannot lie
I stared, looking for meaning in yours
Yearning to ask the questions I couldn't verbalize
Not trusting to be answered truthfully

A sweet and painful layover of star-crossed paths
Casual conversation

Straining with the depth of underpinnings
Just a dash of psychological disposition

As if forces beyond the earthly plane
Had begun to spin a weaving web of desire
So intense, a fire raging untended
Unstoppable, cleansing all in its path

As I laid freshly inked, in your bed
Not touching, but in a room as hot as the tension between us
Invisible barrier screaming caution between
Tossing and turning as if to shake it off
I wondered if you could feel the energy too

I couldn't,
I just couldn't tell you.
What if you laughed, were silent or even worse?
Direct eye contact in that brief moment
Between chaos and quiet
And said, "come on Nicole, what did you expect?"

Little to no recognition
Unready, I realized
Too lost in your own tasty ego sauce
Drowning in bad influences with no filter

You were going to have to break your own heart
Using that girl as a tool for your own destruction
I, being the bystander who couldn't look away
Reluctantly leaned in to hug you
The only time our two bodies had touched
Not wanting to pull away
Yet fearing what kind of portal I was being pulled into

I felt so helpless
Swallowing my pride and selfish thoughts
Sticking in my throat creating the first barrier
It was never really about who won or lost
Each to suffer the same uneasy fate

Anger wasn't my friend here
Silence was both my friend and enemy
Taunting my willpower in each empty moment
I had to learn how to make peace with both

The contract demands both recognize
Running away was the option I took
But you opened the door
Lodged a wedge nice and tight between the ground
Left open, only watching from a far
Never crossing any inappropriate walls
I wouldn't let you
Your pride toed the line hard
My mind and heart needed to get right
For when fate decided to steer this train back
I would be ready this time

THE CONSISTENT QUESTION

What is love?
Is there even a consensus of what is all contains?
Styles and types
Levels of connection
What comprises to become deeper
More intensely held in our hearts
Patience for someone who isn't quite on the same page?
Definitely not an ultimatum or forcing of certain behaviors.
Deeper understanding for something done a different way?
Embracing a success or win even if it doesn't belong to you?
It's messy for sure
Confusing and rewarding at the same time
Shifting and changing your prospective on what is important.
Flawed in many aspects
Defined, undefined and living in a headspace unspoken
Doesn't live up to magazine covers, tabloids or gossip
It's real; real emotion, gritty and uncomfortable
A deeper knowing or acknowledgment of what really is there for you
Boundaries or unbounded in between those who agreed
There is vulnerability and seeing things that was once judged before
Watching someone make a mistake
Knowing the pain, it will cause and committing to help pick up the pieces after
Snotted up nose and tears wiped away
A warm embrace with our expectations
Complete lack of control over another
It's trust that what is put in, will come out
Not here to win an award or brag to a friend
No empty promises or grandiose gestures of appeasement
Chaos and harmony wrapped together
Twisting and flowing further into the unknown
A promise to be authentic in all you do
A hope for a better future outcome
Yet sitting with what is in the here and now
No schematic or blueprint
Just some blind faith and a bit of magik
Starting each day as a brand new shiny open path.

TAKING NAMES

Those whose names we know
You have been here for us all along
But who really are you?
That is for only you to know
For when you lived with us
They didn't notice you
Did you breathe the air I did?
Laughed right along beside me?
Languished in the waves?
Or have you shifted me
Into next of kind consciousness
Because I felt safe
Because I felt whole
You smiled at me
And I knew you
At least I thought
I was confident and self-assured
Your eyes holding me in grace
I couldn't hold you
Not in my arms
But in the idea that moments are temporary
That here in the time
Mere seconds
Shared between us
That time existed much deeper
Extended paces of boundaryless light
This is where I could breathe again

AGAIN

If I ever see you again,
I will show you
How I feel.
Live in wait
Those stolen moments,
Wherein I peeked
Within.
Naked.
So naked.
Before your body
souls to be seen,
Such honesty
Seeped in.
This way and that.
All I wanted to see
Was your success,
Your happiness.
Words sometimes
Not nearly enough,
For such passion
Raging inside.
I want your expression,
Coat me with some fine flannel.
Laughter ringing in the wind.
Staring at me,
Speaking so subtle
But soft.
Whispered the truth
With your eyes.
Laying the path
Brick by brick,
In my hearts path,
To ultimate dominion.
King of kings
Don't you hide who you are.

Tell me,
How much you desire
Such royalty
To hold your heart.
Through this mysterious,
Wildly ambiguous
Destiny of life.
No distance,
Is truly between us.
When once we agreed,
To find one another
Over and over
Again

Printed in the United States
by Baker & Taylor Publisher Services